WHY ARE WE HERE?

EDWIN C. TALBOT

Why Are We Here?

Copyright © 2021 by Edwin C. Talbot.

Paperback ISBN: 978-1-63812-059-9
Ebook ISBN: 978-1-63812-060-5

All rights reserved. No part in this book may be produced and transmitted in any form or by any means, electronic, or mechanical, including photocopying, recording, or by any information storage and retrieval system, without permission in writing from the copyright owner.

The views expressed in this work are solely those of the author and do not necessarily reflect the views of the publisher hereby disclaims any responsibility for them.

Published by Pen Culture Solutions   06/29/2021

Pen Culture Solutions
1-888-727-7204 (USA)
1-800-950-458 (Australia)
support@penculturesolutions.com

INTRODUCTION

For me to continue on my Christian journey it became imperative that I understood why God created the universe and why he placed us here. When considering the struggles, suffering and corruption this world is faced with. The enigma of balancing His love with the realities of the hideous behaviour of some of the members of His creation. He began to loom to me as an ogre playing games with us. I needed to know the truth, in order to make sense of who He really is. In my walk with Him I have found that He will provide the truth, even though I was, in some cases, not able to really deal with it and was quite sorry I had asked the question. We need to remember that we as humans rarely accept the truth and are generally afraid of it. He is no respecter of persons and so it is of little importance as to who asks the question. He will reply to those who seek the truth, if the individual has mischief in their heart there will be no reply. He has never had a problem disclosing any question I have had to ask, on the condition that my intent was not to cause mischief, in other words, if the intent is to win an argument God is not going to provide the individual with the means to laud it over his brother. There are other occasions where I am not meant to know the answer. He just does not answer, and I accept that, however this has occurred in only very few cases. Below is the answer I received from Him on this matter, and it has provided me with enormous peace and blessing. The intent in writing this seemingly small contribution is to share this blessing with all who want it. It is not meant to convince or persuade anyone of anything.

The journey we are about to take starts with the acceptance of a loving, omniscient, and omnipotent God and that the Bible is His message to us in which He says "this is who I AM". You may not be of this persuasion, if so! I still encourage you to read on, if not just for interest, sake.

The question of "why we are here?" and "what are we here for?" is a question that has plagued mankind from creation.

Transience of the Universe

When we consider the transience of nature and of the universe which includes the earth. The pointlessness of it all really strikes home, and we sit with King Solomon in Ecclesiastes when he says, "Vanity of vanities, all is vanity." Meaning that it is all pointless. That everything around us is finite (has a beginning and an end). All levels of scientific, philosophical and religious sectors agree that this universe has a finite beginning and will have a finite end. Thousands of years of learning and development will come to nothing, trillions of lives will have come and gone with no evidence that shows that they ever existed, especially, when this universe comes to an end. If we could find anyone who is 125 years old it would be headline news, The oldest known living individual at the time of writing is 117 years old (verified on 12 February 2020). If asked how many people, numbering in the trillions, who have passed through this world could be remembered, it is surprising how few in number are remembered. So! there is no permanence in anything here on earth.

Having established the generally accepted concept that the universe in fact had a starting point. science would have us believe that the universe started with a big bang generated by a "Singularity" (a euphemism for not knowing what caused it, and why or how a nothing exploded forming the universe). The biblical narrative is not at odds with the suddenness of its beginnings, in fact the truth of the "Big Bang" is miniscule in comparison to what it was like when God spoke it into existence, so the sudden event, is not in dispute. What is in dispute is the "who" or "what" because if there was something there to explode then someone or something put it there in the first place. God Spoke the universe into being (hence the suddenness of the event), and as absurd as that may sound, I consider the opposite of nothing becoming something without any intelligence behind It and resulting in such a well-ordered system with all the incredible complexities and working synergistically, really is an impossible event.

The genesis account is clear on the matter that the universe was in fact a void, nothing whatsoever existed – that the material realm (that is all material matter that can be seen, felt, or detected) did not exist in any form

> *Gen 1:1-2*
>
> *In the beginning God created the Heaven and the earth.*
>
> *2 And the earth was without **form, and void**; and darkness was upon the face of the deep. And the Spirit of God moved upon the face of the waters .KJV*

(Strongs OT:922 - VOID)

(OT:922 <START HEBREW>WhB)

<END HEBREW> bohuw (bo'-hoo); from an unused root (meaning to be empty); a vacuity, i.e. (superficially) an undistinguishable ruin:

KJV - emptiness, void.)

(Biblesoft's New Exhaustive Strong's Numbers and Concordance with Expanded Greek-Hebrew Dictionary. Copyright © 1994, 2003, 2006 Biblesoft, Inc. and International Bible Translators, Inc.)

Accepting the Genesis account of creation, it makes this universe only around 10-20,000 years old, then the question is "Why a God existing in an eternal spiritual realm, would create a physical realm, of such exquisite physical beauty, along with all its violence, suffering and destruction?" Especially when it is of such a relatively temporary design.

When posed with this question members of the clergy normally respond as follows:-

- ***It was worth it*** – my response is "to whom was it worth it and what is the worth?"

- ***It is a testing ground for us*** – This is a ludicrous conclusion as the final outcome for each of us was recorded from the foundation of the world, long before any of us were born.

    (Rev 17:8 The beast that thou sawest was, and is not; and shall ascend out of the bottomless pit, and go into perdition: and they that dwell on the earth shall wonder, **whose names were not written in the book of life from the foundation of the world,** *when they behold the beast that was, and is not, and yet is. KJV)*

- ***It was for Gods Pleasure*** – this concept is even more ludicrous unless God is particularly masochistic, or else be considered a complete failure in His endeavours – as it cost Him the life of His Son, to redeem the world and the people in it, which I cannot consider being a particularly pleasing experience.

- Another option is that He is sadistically playing games with us like a cat with a mouse – as said previously that He already knows the final outcome. (the failure, suffering and death of us all).

So there would, seemingly, be no purpose in creating a world such as this.

Considering the above we have the scriptural quotation below that would seem to be even more absurd:

John 3:15-16

15 That whosoever believeth in him should not perish, but have eternal life.

16 ***For God so loved the world, that he gave his only begotten Son***, that whosoever believeth in him should not perish, but have everlasting life. KJV

The absurdity comes from the idea that He made the world and the universe only to have to redeem it (buy it back) through the death of His Son. A provision made prior to the start of the creation.

This famous scripture challenges us to now consider the above to be either the truth or a lie: If a lie, then we are all without hope and there is no point to life whatever.

If the statement is true then we are faced with the dilemma.

Why would an all knowing loving eternal God place us here knowing that we are going to fall and that our situation was going to be so hopeless that he was going to have to send His Son to be a sacrifice for us as a means to redeem us (buy us back) in order to restore our acceptability to God?

That He would create this massive universe (relative to ourselves) and in the midst of this create this little jewel (the Earth) that in contrast to the rest is so utterly miniscule as to have no significance at all. If the earth exploded tomorrow it would have no effect on any other part of the universe whatsoever (except perhaps the moon).

So here we are, utterly insignificant little beings running around on an equally insignificant little planet, spinning around an insignificant sun, **going absolutely nowhere**, and each of us will do it for about 70 years.

The enormity of this God is displayed if we go and examine the creation and the incredible attention to detail regarding the design of the universe and His creation of life. We are faced with a mind bogglingly powerful, awesome Person with astronomical intelligence.

It is for this reason that one astronomer studying the heavens through the telescope, came to the conclusion that God's existence was doubtful and if He did exist, then the level of our insignificance was such that He could not possibly have any interest in us. God then took him through the microscope, and he saw the same level of order through the microscope as he did through the telescope. His conclusion was that "God is the God of the infinitely great and the God of the infinitely small. However the infinitely small, is greater than the infinitely great because the infinitely great is made up of the infinitely small". God's power and intelligence is to be found wherever we choose to look.

So again the question is asked: "Why would someone such as this create a transient realm, which relative to Himself, is so temporary?"

This would indicate that He is either extremely impractical or perhaps there could be another reason altogether regarding His purpose for creating the physical realm.

In order to explore this idea further we now need to examine the economy of Satan.

THE INTRODUCTION OF GOOD AND EVIL

The start of it all

Gen 2:9

And out of the ground made the Lord God to grow every tree that is pleasant to the sight, and good for food; the tree of life also in the midst of the garden, and the tree of knowledge of good and evil.

Gen 2:16-17

16 And the Lord God commanded the man, saying, Of every tree of the garden thou mayest freely eat:

17 But of the tree of the knowledge of good and evil, thou shalt not eat of it: for in the day that thou eatest thereof thou shalt surely die.

If we consider that prior to eating the fruit from the tree described above (it was not an apple by the way) Adam and Eve could not commit sin as they had no knowledge of what it was – just as it is with the rest of creation – the wild animals have no conscience and therefore have no knowledge of what is right or wrong – they just do as circumstances and instinct dictate without any further consideration. The scriptures indicate that man was created with this same freedom – The moment they partook of this fruit, "their eyes were opened" and therefore came to know the difference (between good and evil, right and wrong). He immediately came under bondage to his own conscience, now causing the inner turmoil of being, daily, pulled and pushed by these two forces. People think that if only they could make God go away they would be able to free themselves of this bondage.

What is fascinating about the Adam and Eve narrative is the question of good and evil entering into the conversation so early in the bible narrative. We know that the bible manuscripts are very old and date back to a time where the philosophical arguments regarding "good" and "evil" had not yet eventuated. Yet we have this account showing that God provided the potential for their introduction right from the beginning, and that Adam and Eve were not aware of what they meant.

If the writer of the book of Genesis did not have the inspiration of God at his disposal I could not imagine that he would have come up with the concept of these opposing forces being introduced as described – because he would have taken them for granted as we do now. They are so much part of our psyche that normal people do not stop to give the matter a second thought, we automatically make judgements regarding the rights and wrongs on events taking place around us all the time.

The modern concept of Relativism

We know that the scriptures of Genesis preceded the first forms of philosophy (Ethics) which gave rise to the ideas of what really constitutes right and wrong behaviour. This philosophical thinking introduced the idea of **Relativism** (that nothing is right or wrong of itself but only as it relates to you or those around you – what is right for you may not correspondingly apply to someone else) hence generating a study in this particular form of ethics, culminates in the question of who ultimately decides on "What is good and what is evil"? For in the finality, (they say) "there are no absolutes."

Definition of relativism from Stanford Encyclopedia of philosophy

Author & Citation Info | Friends PDF Preview | InPho Search | PhilPapers Bibliography

Relativism

First published Sun Feb 2, 2003

Relativism is not a **single doctrine** but a family of views whose common theme is that some central aspect of experience, thought, evaluation, or even reality is somehow relative to something else. For example standards of justification, moral principles or truth are sometimes said to be relative to language, culture, or biological makeup. Although relativistic lines of thought often lead to very ***implausible conclusions***, there is something seductive about them, and they have captivated a wide range of thinkers from a wide range of traditions.

Conscience

However: The scriptures clear up all these debates with what is as obvious as our noses on our faces and that is that we are born with a God given conscience

Dictionary definition for *conscience*

(con·science

noun

1. the inner sense of what is right or wrong in one's conduct or motives, impelling one toward right action: to follow the dictates of conscience.

2. the complex of ethical and moral principles that controls or inhibits the actions or thoughts of an individual.

3. an inhibiting sense of what is prudent: I'd eat another piece of pie but my conscience would bother me.

4. conscientiousness.

5. Obsolete. consciousness; self-knowledge.

So the struggle with what or who determines what is really good or evil goes on in endless debate.

God allowed men to attempt to live only guided by their conscience. It became clear after a relatively short time that they were unable to effectively live in this manner, with the result that people began to lead such evil lives that God had to take drastic action to clean the earth up. So He cleaned the world up with a gigantic flood covering the whole earth. It needed a more stringent set of guidelines to determine direction for their lives, so God started with a two-way communication system, namely priests and prophets.

The instructions went from God to the people via the prophets and from the people to God via the priest.

This process It must be remembered that once the law (which is really just a confirmation of their conscience) came into being it was absolute. The individual stands guilty before God for any transgression of that law. And when we consider law No1:

> Matt 22:36-37
>
> 36 Master, which is the great commandment in the law?
>
> 37 Jesus said unto him, Thou shalt love the Lord thy God with all thy heart, and with all thy soul, and with all thy mind. KJV

It is with consternation that we will find that there is no one that has kept this law – nevertheless it is on the same page as the law that says do not kill or steal, and we must remember that God is not a god of degrees, there is no such thing as a little or big transgression. The result being:

> *Ezek 18:4*
>
> *4 Behold,* **all souls are mine***; as the soul of the father, so also the soul of the son is mine: the soul that sinneth, it shall die.*
>
> *KJV*

We must now conclude that we are all sinners and stand guilty before the living God and will face eternal damnation unless there is some intervention on our behalf for mercy or GRACE.

BIBLICAL ACCOUNT OF MAN'S REBELLION AGAINST GOD'S LAWS

(consider the quotation from Psalm 2

(Ps 2:1-4

1 Why do the heathen rage, and the people imagine a vain thing?

2 The kings of the earth set themselves, and the rulers take counsel together, against the Lord, and against his anointed, saying,

3 Let us break their bands asunder, and cast away their cords from us. (KJV).

Today we have the culmination of the above statement. These forces that have prevailed through history, men have sought to undermine God's authority through every part of history.

We will deal in detail with the majority of this when we examine Satan's plan to subjugate the inhabitants of this world.

> *The kings of the earth set themselves, and the rulers take counsel together, against the Lord, and against his anointed, saying,*

This literally means that the world powers conspire against God and His Christ.

The UN of today is in fact a perfect fulfillment of this prophecy – the removal of prayers in Schools, So called personal freedoms etc. this is In fact the push to remove God and His Christ from all events in our daily lives.

But needless to say regarding the description of the world's powers in Psalm 2 v. 3 is the attempt to find a release from what they consider as "The massive restrictions and guilt producing constraints placed by **"the church"**.

Let us break their bands asunder – Lets break the ropes that are constraining us – The ropes that the world considers is constraining them are the rules imposed by their own conscience, that if they could only get rid of them they would experience real freedom and true happiness. Let us break these ropes and throw them off us. The amazing thing about this is that it is like the ship's captain standing on the deck of his ship and tossing all his charts and navigational aids over the side and saying "now I am free to go wherever I please" little realizing that he is bound to be destroyed by the first set of rocks that come his way.

Satan's Subjugation of the World Population

When we consider the resolutions and laws relating to human rights, we are bombarded with rules and law changes that leave the strongest among us trembling and confused. The irrational decisions and direction leave us so nonplussed that we think that they could not possibly be serious, so we do not take them seriously and then we are suddenly faced with the reality and consequences of those laws and rules in our midst. We seem to be blind to the fact that whole of the world powers are driven to meet Satan's purpose of bringing the world's human population into his subjugation (they are not even aware that they are being used in this way, they honestly believe that in some perverted way they are acting in the best interest of the people). Satan will do anything in his power to separate us as far from God as possible.

All of this results in uncontrollable crime waves, bands of gangs that are almost totally out of control. Teachers who are too afraid to reprimand children in the class, in fear of being physically injured by the students in question. Parents who are too afraid to discipline their children, as the children, have been informed by the school that if their parents punish them then the child should invoke their rights and report the matter to the school or police. Pornography of the most graphic nature freely available to children of all ages (I could go on for hours here). As a consequence, this is having devastating results for some of the parents. In short people are living in increasing states of fear and really do not know who to turn to. The government blame them for losing control of their children and yet they face punishment if they try to impose discipline. Everyone is complaining about the state of the youth and all seem to be powerless to do anything about it.

A large amount of time and space could be allocated to the consequences of UN resolutions, Human Rights legislation and The World Council of Churches, together with faceless government Bureaucracies. When we look at the anarchist we see a growing group that are bent on removing restrictive laws and so contradict the laws of God. However, I think that most of us are aware of most of those issues at hand. What we need to keep in mind is that this is Satan's tool to make himself "Like the Most High" He believes that once mankind has been subjected to his will and living lives as far from God's will as possible, he will have arrived.

We can see that the road the world powers are taking is juxtaposed to God and His leading – The world is almost in complete rebellion against God.

When we consider the narrative of nearly every story written we find that it has as its center the struggle between these two factors. There is almost without exception the "good guy" and the "bad guy" and generally to our relief the good guy wins. We cannot think outside of this square.

The prevailing question pervading all this is WHY did God do it this way? Stop and think for a second – is there anywhere else in the universe that sin exists – **no!** *Only in people's minds.* All indications are that the whole of the creation is totally obedient to God's will. It would appear that in the mind of mankind is the only place in the entire creation that has the ability to say "NO!" to God and the only one lacking in good sense to do so.

From Genesis 2:16 God does not elaborate on why Adam will die if He eats the fruit of the tree of Knowledge of good and evil. In fact! it was not a physical death (he lived for more than 900 years after the event) what He was talking about was spiritual death – causing a separation between them and God. (God is a spiritual being and if we are spiritually dead then there is no means of communication with Him), consider this analogy – You are in a physical condition where you have lost all five senses. You cannot feel, see, taste, smell or hear then although you are alive, for you the world does not exist because you have no way of contacting anyone or anything in it. You are in fact dead to the world. So it is with us in the spiritual realm we have lost the means of communicating in that realm so we are dead to it. Additionally, the scriptures indicate that, sin cannot enter the presence of God, so they were now cut off from their creator and totally at the mercy of Satan. This is what was in the dire warning when God instructed them not to eat of that tree. We have, through Adam, entered the conflict between God and Satan and the battle ground is our minds. God Has provided the scenario that has played out over the past 10,000 years. He has provided the human race with a free will and has allowed it to express itself in all ways possible. So we cannot blame Him for the way that some people have chosen to exercise that free will. This means that at the end of it all when the judgment seat is set, God will Bring all those things done in secret out into the open and the final judgment will begin.

Rev 20:11-12

11 And I saw a great white throne, and him that sat on it, from whose face the earth and the heaven fled away; and there was found no place for them.

12 And I saw the dead, small and great, stand before God; and the books were opened: and another book was opened, which is the book of life: and the dead were judged out of those things which were written in the books, according to their works. KJV

All will be revealed on how that free will was exercised and the bringing to account will start. God will not allow us to use Satan as an excuse for what we have done, but will nevertheless hold him to account for the deceptions he has played out on us

Rev 20:10

10 And the devil that deceived them was cast into the lake of fire and brimstone, where the beast and the false prophet are, and shall be tormented day and night for ever and ever. KJV

Satan's plan to "become like the most high"

(Isa 14:12-14

2 How art thou fallen from heaven, O Lucifer, son of the morning! how art thou cut down to the ground, which didst weaken the nations!

13 For thou hast said in thine heart, I will ascend into heaven, I will exalt my throne above the stars of God: I will sit also upon the mount of the congregation, in the sides of the north:

14 I will ascend above the heights of the clouds; I will be like the most High. KJV)

This plan is, and always has been, in process to accomplish this end which is to bring all mankind under his subjugation. He has spent the last 6,000 years working on turning the inhabitants of the earth away from God and uses:-

- Money (Commerce)
- Power
- Pleasure
- Science
- Religion
- Sex
- Competition (God in no way encourages any form of competition)

This is by no means a comprehensive list as there are other tools in his arsenal, and using these he has now almost completely succeeded in turning people's hearts and minds away from God – The majority of the people in the world have come to the point that they will believe anything that is proffered in the Name of Science no matter how absurd it may be, or how it lacks in true evidence or how many times it has been shown to be incorrect. This is indicative of the level of "faith" they now place in science in preference to God.

If we consider that it is commerce that the bible is referring to as "Mystery Babylon The Great" (in Revelation 17) The Mother of Harlots and the description provided regarding Babylon in Revelation 18. She is portrayed as having deluded all the peoples, powers and nations and they have come under the power of her fornication. (I do cover this in my previous book "Where on Earth are we going") Then we can see that Satan has seduced people to the extent that the general population have willingly enslaved themselves to generating personal wealth, status, and the consequential pleasures. Their delusion is realized when they are left wondering where all their dreams and aspirations have gone. Because they have not been able to devote any time for anything else, other than getting up in the morning, going to work and coming home at night exhausted, only to get up again the next day and do it all again. They do not have the time or inclination to check the truth of what the media are presenting to them with, so they just accept it all at face value (of science or political agendas). In fact it is largely through the entertainment field (television) that they are bombarded with indoctrination. Applied when they are tired and thereby providing the greatest level of traction on their mental attitudes. These are the very techniques used to inflict the Pavlovian mind control in the early soviet communism indoctrination process (referred to at the time as brainwashing). They would daily work the population to the point of exhaustion and before they were allowed to go home and rest they would be required to attend government controlled indoctrination sessions. This process has been refined to a precise science, resulting in the general population being unaware of what is being done to them. So piece by piece Satan has succeeded in eroding their/our freedoms, freedoms that were provided by God in the first place.

Satan's enslavement of the population

Satan has achieved the level of slavery in the population today that boggles the mind. He has us wrapped up in the daily slog of commerce where our individualism is totally consumed in order to "earn money" and, virtually, the total amount earned is committed just to maintaining our "life styles". We do not make or grow anything ourselves and are totally dependent on the products produced by other forms of commerce, and they in turn are only interested in the gathering of wealth and have no, or very little concern of how the products being manufactured affect those using them.

The level of slavery is stupendous when we realize that through, government taxation, we are working between one to two days a week (at best) for the government. If you consider all levels of taxation imposed, by governments, you will be astonished at just how many days each week you are working just for the government to put the funds into their coffers with very little, or no benefit to yourself. However, we still convince ourselves that "WE ARE FREE".

We are now facing the terrifying concept of "Genetically Modified Foods" and the company manufacturing them has been allowed to patent the life form that has resulted. This means that they own the food and any farmer whose crop has become contaminated with the seeds of the modified crop has to pay royalties to the company owning the crop and are not permitted to use their own seed to replant but are now forced to buy the seed from the company. They have accomplished the removal of all freedom of farmers to develop and farm their own products.

This brings us to another level of control where companies having this level of power will finally control all food producing crops. The original crops were produced and patented under the auspices of benefitting mankind by making crops of higher yields and were more resistant to disease. In fact, all of it is only in the interest and benefit to the company who patented them and to control the world's food production thereby controlling the people.

If all the above, isn't enough the battle for fresh water is gaining in intensity. If we were required to pay the price for petrol that we are paying for a bottle of water, there would be an almighty outcry. So once Satan has gained control over commerce the food and water - his control on humanity is almost complete.

> ***Rev 13:16-18***
>
> ***And he causeth all, both small and great, rich and poor, free and bond, to receive a mark in their right hand, or in their foreheads:***
>
> ***17 And that no man might buy or sell, save he that had the mark, or the name of the beast, or the number of his name.***

18 Here is wisdom. Let him that hath understanding count the number of the beast: for it is the number of a man; and his number is Six hundred threescore and six. KJV

I think that we can now see that Satan has a clear plan of subjugating all the people of this world and he is step by step bringing this plan to fruition. The finality will be when the whole of commerce is brought under his control and no one will be able to trade lest they have his permission in the form of a mark in the hand or forehead. They will not be able to even grow their own food.

INNOCENCE OF HEAVEN

We now need to deal with a paradox that requires our attention. Because Satan is present with God at the start of creation – else he could not have been there to tempt Eve. So, Satan's, so called fall has to have taken place prior to the story of Job being written, which is recognized as the oldest book in the bible. The question therefore exists as to whether "Satan has sinned?" If we answer 'yes', then the further question is, how does he have access to God as described below?

Job 1:5-10

*6 Now there was a day when the sons of God came to present themselves before the Lord, **and Satan** came also among them.*

7 And the Lord said unto Satan, Whence comest thou? Then Satan answered the Lord, and said, From going to and fro in the earth, and from walking up and down in it.

8 And the Lord said unto Satan, Hast thou considered my servant Job, that there is none like him in the earth, a perfect and an upright man, one that feareth God, and escheweth evil?

9 Then Satan answered the Lord, and said, Doth Job fear God for nought?

10 Hast not thou made an hedge about him, and about his house, and about all that he hath on every side? thou hast blessed the work of his hands, and his substance is increased in the land.

Job 2:1-3

Again there was a day when the sons of God came to present themselves before the Lord, and **Satan came** *also among them to present himself before the Lord.*

2 And the Lord said unto Satan, From whence comest thou? And Satan answered the Lord, and said, From going to and fro in the earth, and from walking up and down in it.

3 And the Lord said unto Satan, Hast thou considered my servant Job, that there is none like him in the earth, a perfect and an upright man, one that feareth God, and escheweth evil? and still he holdeth fast his integrity, although thou movedst me against him, to destroy him without cause. KJV

Satan is only cast out of heaven at the end as depicted in the book of Revelation below.

Rev 12:7-12

7 And there was war in heaven: Michael and his angels fought against the dragon; and the dragon fought and his angels,

8 And prevailed not; neither was their place found any more in heaven.

9 And the great dragon was cast out, that old serpent, called the Devil, and Satan, which deceiveth the whole world: he was cast out into the earth, and his angels were cast out with him.

10 And I heard a loud voice saying in heaven, Now is come salvation, and strength, and the kingdom of our God, and the power of his Christ: for the accuser of our brethren is cast down, **which accused them before our God day and night**.

11 And they overcame him by the blood of the Lamb, and by the word of their testimony; and they loved not their lives unto the death.

12 Therefore rejoice, ye heavens, and ye that dwell in them. Woe to the inhabiters of the earth and of the sea! for the devil is come down unto you, having great wrath, because he knoweth that he hath but a short time. KJV

Most Christians pass over these verses without really questioning them. There is need to contemplate the fact that if Satan had sin in him, he would not be able to come into the presence of God. It must be remembered that God cannot abide sin in His presence – if sin could come into the presence of God, then why would the sacrifice of Jesus Christ have been necessary?

The fact that Satan could openly walk into God's presence as depicted in Job we are left with no other conclusion that up to now NO SIN has been appropriated to him YET.

As explained earlier sin can only exist here on earth and is appropriated at the judgement. (side note, if we had to wait for the judgement to take place and our declaration of guilt made. It would have been too late to apply grace.)

The appropriation of sin comes with the judgement – when Jesus came to this earth, He did it willingly:

> Isa 6:8
>
> *8 Also I heard the voice of the Lord, saying, Whom shall I send, and who will go for us? Then said I, Here am I; send me. KJV*

So, then we are presented with concept that Jesus took His incarnation upon himself willingly –entering the world in the normal way as a little baby. (The concept of the creator of this universe entering this world as a helpless baby is beyond comprehension.) And then living an exemplary life is without dispute.

Satan, on the other hand is cast out of heaven and cast into the earth at the very end and indications are that he is extremely angry and sets about taking revenge about being confined within a human body as Christ was. The point here is that we are presented with a most unusual fact that he now possesses a body that had pre-existed and is therefore in its resurrected form. Satan is not subjected to the ignominy of having to develop from a baby. It will be the first time in history (other than Adam and Eve) that an individual appears on earth as an adult and in this case arises out of the bottomless pit.

Jesus was judged

All those in the form of human flesh will pass through judgement. Jesus Christ was judged in the following way and in all cases was found "Not Guilty" on all counts. Judgements were as follows:

- **By God** -Luke 3:22

    22 And the Holy Ghost descended in a bodily shape like a dove upon him, and a voice came from heaven, which said, ***Thou art my beloved Son; in thee I am well pleased. KJV***

- **By man**

Pilate was the representative of the most powerful nation on the earth and below is his judgement on Jesus that he confirms three times

    -John 18:38

    38 Pilate saith unto him, What is truth? And when he had said this, he went out again unto the Jews, and saith unto them, ***I find in him no fault at all. KJV***

- **By Satan** -Mark 5:7-8

> *7 And cried with a loud voice, and said, What have I to do with thee, **Jesus, thou Son of the most high God?** I adjure thee by God, that thou torment me not.*
>
> *8 For he said unto him, Come out of the man, thou unclean spirit. KJV*

Satan is Judged (having been forced into a body of flesh) by God at the end and there is no need of any other judgement as God's Judgement is final.

We define the place where God resides as "Heaven" and there is no issue with this, however we should take into account that it is really the spiritual realm that we are focused on. We are a soul which is a separate entity from our body and spirit. It is through the physical body that we exist and interact with things on earth and once we experience the new birth into the spirit then our soul (which is who we are) has access to heaven, the spiritual realm, through our spirit by The Holy Spirit. However, being in existence in the physical also, there is continual conflict between the body and spirit for our attention and unfortunately our body (the flesh) usually wins by us giving it preference over the spirit, mainly, due to the fact that the physical has the higher level of influence on us.

Paul indicates that what we can see of the spiritual world can be considered to looking through smoked glass, resulting in our only being able to see shadows.

One of the facts that may astonish most is that no sin can exist in heaven – remember sin only exists in men's minds. It is not possible for the tenants of heaven to sin. The capacity to facilitate it just does not exist. Furthermore, they have access to God's presence where no sin can exist.

We then must realize that Heaven has a stupendously mind boggling, level of innocence. Also, that the members of heaven are eternal beings having access to the presence of God. We who are unable to imagine a world of this nature, have problems contemplating what life will be like. We have images of people on clouds playing harps, and any science fiction stories that try to depict such a place make it look so dreary and boring that no one could possibly want to go there. However, the statement out of the scriptures below absolutely proves otherwise:

1 Cor 2:9

9 But as it is written, Eye hath not seen, nor ear heard, neither have entered into the heart of man, the things which God hath prepared for them that love him.

KJV

The question we need to contemplate is how does God now deal with the situation (with Satan)? As it had to be achieved without allowing sin to enter into this innocent spiritual realm.

When Satan considered challenging God's position. God could no doubt see the potential of where this matter was leading to and needed to deal with it expediently by providing the means for Satan to go about developing this challenge. The matter is complex because in heaven there was no provision for him to make his challenge to gain control. So, he could see that this beautiful creation was tailor made for him to make his move and so doing gain control over this newly created universe, and push God out of the way. This would ultimately reveal his true evil capacity to everyone. To our knowledge this was the "only game in town" so to speak. So, if he was going to make his move it would have to be at that juncture so as to seduce these two innocent simple humans without much trouble.

From all indications, it would seem, that he considers violence and competition as his first course of action to achieve his aims

At this point, it must be remembered, that Satan had not **done** anything wrong: he had only thought it. The question that needs to be answered is; if God had destroyed Satan at the point when these thoughts entered his mind, how would the rest of heaven have reacted to his demise? As he had done nothing wrong, he had only thought it. Would they now serve God in fear or in love? I think most of us can see the answer to this question as the rest of heaven would have seen God destroy someone who has done nothing wrong.

CREATION OF THE PHYSICAL REALM

Working from a spiritual realm and looking at an eternal innocent existence, how does God deal with His dilemma.

I need you to see the brilliance of the person we are dealing with. He decides to create this physical realm with all its incredible intricacies and complexity, He now not only has to take Satan into account when considering this creation but to make the whole thing successful, He needs to create us with a free will in order that we may be able to freely choose between either side. To add to the mix so that we are not unduly influenced, He makes both sides, of the conflict, invisible to the inhabitants of this creation. He creates this realm so stupendously colossal that the pride of the inhabitants, of the insignificant earth, has nowhere to really exercise itself. Fascinatingly enough this does not even slow them down in their utterly futile attempts to "conquer" the universe.

He creates a world perfect for habitation and Himself declares that it is good – I could spend the rest of my life here going through His miraculous design and creation.

We need to see the level of his love here, where He creates the first people in God's image "Lets create man in our image" (Body, Soul and Spirit – the three in one) and He makes them immune to the wiles of Satan by creating them innocent (they have no knowledge of good and evil) so they cannot sin and therefore have built in immunity. The whole earth is then placed under their jurisdiction.

Now God makes one avenue available for Satan to wrest control from them and to start the subjugation of the people of this earth. For this is the manner in which he perceives that he will become like the most high when all the people are under his control. The decision to take part in the conflict between God and Satan is not made by God, He only made it a possibility, it was Adam's decision to willingly partake of the fruit offered by eve. Even at this point Satan has done nothing wrong – the wrong- doing was committed by Adam, Eve and the serpent.

The Earthly Journey

Really importantly, at this point, is to take a good look at the scriptures – which are a collection of divinely inspired writings in which God, over a very wide period, undertook to tell us who He is.

Here things begin to get interesting for as we now consider the scriptures (writings that God has given us, in order to communicate who he is and how we are to go about developing a relationship with Him) and in these writings, it would appear that everything is between man and God, Satan does not appear to take much of a role of any consequence. Added to this, all the books provided in this cannon are the works of members of the Israeli population.

We have God selecting a person (Abraham) and from him He created an entire nation (Israel) the only nation that had its beginnings without a country. And the only nation to be dispersed throughout the world for two thousand years and did not lose its identity (even though they were so hated by nearly all those around them) resulting in them coming back to their land – to the consternation of the World.

The point is that God's message to us is through His people and their land. If we consider the size of Israel and its overall influence over matters of this earth, it can only be considered a paralogism (A violation of logic) as the area of Israel is 0.01365% of the Earths land mass and the population is 0.192% of the Earth's population. Yet the accomplishments of this nation have contributed something in the order of 85% of the major achievements in society, science and arts. This is outside of all reasonable proportion. The influence the Jewish community have over the American politics is huge, which means that the government cannot ignore the impact of the Jewish contingent during elections.

Having said all this, we must realize that this world belongs to Satan, if you have doubts about this have a look at:

> *Luke 4:5-7*
>
> *5 And the devil, taking him up into an high mountain, shewed unto him all the kingdoms of the world in a moment of time.*
>
> *6 And the devil said unto him, All this power will I give thee, and the glory of them:* ***for that is delivered unto me****; and to whomsoever I will I give it.*
>
> *7 If thou therefore wilt worship me, all shall be thine. KJV*

This may come as a surprise to many Christians however, I do believe that if Satan had made an incorrect statement of fact in this regard Jesus would have corrected him regarding the error. Jesus did not! And this confirms the fact of who is in control of this world. God has selected only the tiny little spot (Israel) as His own and through it to let the rest of the world know who He is. Did the people of this region do anything to warrant God's attention – Not that can be seen, as all indications are that they have only rebelled and never complied with his instructions.

It is amazing that if anyone really wants to know who God is – all they have to do is take a long look at the history of Israel

Now it can be seen that God is overt in all his dealing with us, even going so far as to provide a written means of how we might get to know Him. This is in stark contrast with Satan who is covert in all his dealings, it is not in his interest to allow us to know what his plans are.

God has taken the time and trouble to let us know who He is without undertaking to expose Satan. Most references to Satan are merely statements of warning or clarification.

Satan has not provided any means for us to get to know him as he prefers to remain unobserved. However, we see that he stands for everything that is opposed to God.

He destroys all that we call "good" and replaces it with the opposite - he provides every sort of religion just so that we do not turn to Christ. He has a religion to suit everyone, including those who are "not religious" as in the case of evolution. Commerce is the biggest religion today and it has consumed every nation of the world - "No one is free from her vices" and enslaves virtually the entire population of the world.

Unfortunately, his corruption has entered the Christian church to the extent that many too are now focused at using techniques directed at bringing their congregations under control. I think that some churches now have more rules than the ten commandments, which Christ died to free us from.

God says that we are all the same and should be humble seeking to be the least in our community - Satan says be proud, be strong in competition beating all your competition into submission. Funnily enough we see this as the most attractive course of action. When in all this we, actually do see someone behave in a compassionate manner it is celebrated as something special rather than being the norm.

THE POWER OF CHRIST

The power of Christ in our lives; is the freedom He gives us – this freedom is such that even the pastors of the churches are somewhat afraid of it. It threatens to allow things to get "out of control". It actually comes down to the fact that we should only respond to the leaning and direction of Christ and The Holy Spirit, resulting in the body of Christ responding to the head with humility, love and understanding.

> John 8:36
>
> If the Son therefore shall make you free, ye shall be free indeed. KJV

The Power of Satan

Generated by violence, Competition, and hatred. Any studies of those who have been in contact with Satan's realm will know that the position and status you hold in that realm is generated by the status of the demon that controls you.

Satan's power is through subjugation and removal of personal freedoms.

It is amazing to realize that Satan does not seem to contemplate anything other than violence to achieve his ends. Even at the very end when he is released from the bottomless pit – he goes about to gather the peoples of this earth, who have enjoyed a thousand years of peace, to do battle with Christ. He has no other vehicle to use, other than violence.

ATTRIBUTES OF FAITH

The main portals through which God and Satan gain access to our lives is through the process of Belief (faith) it is through this avenue that we open channels to either God or Satan to operate.

Faith in the English language has a meaning that would seem to be somewhat obscure

The bible's account of what it means is determined by the context of the scriptures identifying it. There are very few references to the word in the Old Testament in contrast to the number of references in the New Testament.

> *Deut 32:20*
>
> *20 And he said, I will hide my face from them, I will see what their end shall be: for they are a very froward generation, children in whom is no faith. KJV*

OT:529 Faith

OT:529 <START HEBREW>/Wma@

<END HEBREW> 'emuwn (ay-moon'); from OT:539; established, i.e. (figuratively) trusty; also (abstractly) trustworthiness:

KJV - faith (-ful), truth.

(Biblesoft's New Exhaustive Strong's Numbers and Concordance with Expanded Greek-Hebrew Dictionary. Copyright © 1994, 2003, 2006 Biblesoft, Inc. and International Bible Translators, Inc.)

Heb 11:1

11 Now faith is the substance of things hoped for, the evidence of things not seen. KJV

NT:4102

<START GREEK>pi/sti$

<END GREEK> pistis (pis'-tis); from NT:3982; persuasion, i.e. credence; moral conviction (of religious truth, or the truthfulness of God or a religious teacher), especially reliance upon Christ for salvation; abstractly, constancy in such profession; by extension, the system of religious (Gospel) truth itself:

KJV - assurance, belief, believe, faith, fidelity.

(Biblesoft's New Exhaustive Strong's Numbers and Concordance with Expanded Greek-Hebrew Dictionary. Copyright © 1994, 2003, 2006 Biblesoft, Inc. and International Bible Translators, Inc.)

Oxford Dictionary defines faith as:

Faith

[feyth] Show IPA

noun

1. confidence or trust in a person or thing: faith in another's ability.

2. belief that is not based on proof: He had faith that the hypothesis would be substantiated by fact.

3. belief in God or in the doctrines or teachings of religion the firm faith of the Pilgrims.

4. belief in anything, as a code of ethics, standards of merit, etc.: to be of the same faith with someone concerning honesty.

5. a system of religious belief: the Christian faith; the Jewish faith.

It is little wonder that people misinterpret the meaning in the scriptures when the word faith is used. As most people seem to see it as meaning the system of religion rather than an absolute level of trust.

Having covered all the details above, let's look at practical methodologies of invoking faith as a form of trust. It is believing in something or someone without any form of doubt. The moment doubt enters the equation faith does not exist.

Jesus to Peter when he tried to walk on the water with Jesus:

> Matt 14:31
>
> *31 And immediately Jesus stretched forth his hand, and caught him, and said unto him,* **O thou of little faith, wherefore didst thou doubt?** *KJV*

Again, when Jesus cursed the fig tree and it died:

> Matt 21:21
>
> *21 Jesus answered and said unto them, Verily I say unto you,* **If ye have faith, and doubt not**, *ye shall not only do this which is done to the fig tree, but also if ye shall say unto this mountain, Be thou removed, and be thou cast into the sea; it shall be done. KJV*

The main issue we are establishing here is that when we are looking for God's intervention in our lives, God delivers through the channels we open up by faith

Satan's access to our lives is the same except that with God it is normally a conscious action. In contrast, for example, when we are watching movies and the situation in the plot becomes extreme, we find the level of anxiety growing, which is only alleviated with the advent of the story's hero. On the hero's arrival we normally feel a sense that all will be well now that he/she is there. This manifestation of misplaced faith is what we are faced with, on a daily basis.

Satan can gain access to various parts of our lives through this same mechanism – without our even knowing it.

On the other hand, we have become so discouraged by being disappointed at every turn we feel that we don't dare put our trust in anyone because they will fail. When we grow up aligning Christmas with an old man living at the North pole giving out gifts to those who have been "GOOD", and Easter is aligned to a bunny rabbit hiding Easter eggs. Only to realise that they are fantasy, why would we think our children would consider Jesus to be anything other than a fantasy for Jesus is on the same page as Santa Claus and the Easter Bunny.

Misplaced trust includes our:

- hopes and trust we have in our governments – that no matter how much they have failed us in the past, that somehow, they will finally get it right.

- Hopes and trust in the economy – no matter how many stock market, crashes and economic depressions we see and experience. Somehow, we will be all right if we just have enough in the bank to see us through.

    As an example, to this fallacy, we can look at the situation in Zimbabwe – (which is not that different to Germany in 1929)

    HARARE, Zimbabwe, April 25 — How bad is inflation in Zimbabwe? Well, consider this: at a supermarket near the center of this tatterdemalion capital, toilet paper costs $417.

    No, not per roll. Four hundred seventeen Zimbabwean dollars is the value of a single two-ply sheet. A roll costs $145,750 — in American currency, about 69 cents.

> *Therefore a person who was truly a millionaire in Zimbabwe in the year 2000 now has a fortune worth not much more than one American dollar today.*

- Placing our trust in other people who have done little or nothing to warrant that trust, other than making promises which are seldom realised.

These are the mechanisms that Satan uses to diminish our ability to truly have faith in anything. We are let down so often and regularly that doubt would seem to be the only consistent state of mind we live in today.

Conclusion

Where does all this lead us to?

It would seem that Satan does not succeed in subjugating all the peoples of this planet and will cause nations like China and her allies to oppose him and move towards the west with an army having a size of 200 million which invokes a response through Satan to move all the armies of the west to move eastward to meet the threat and it would seem that they meet in the valley of Megiddo with a conflagration that threatens to destroy the whole world. In Matthew 24 Jesus indicates that if the length of this conflagration was not stopped there would be no flesh left on the face of the earth.

Meanwhile God is pouring out judgement on the earth, the likes of which is unprecedented, using the weather, meteorites, poisoned water etc. All of which is in preparation for Christ's return.

Jesus' return to this earth and Jerusalem is with His people in tow. The scriptural account is that at his arrival (all the world will witness the event) Satan and his hordes will point to Jerusalem and Jesus as the central cause of all the worlds woes and the current predicament. The world's armies will then surround Jerusalem and attempt to do battle with Jesus Christ.

Jesus will step outside Jerusalem and the original scenario will be repeated where He faces the powers of this world, outside Jerusalem, on His own but this time it is their blood that will be shed not His and the bible indicates that the blood will flow as high as the horses bridles for a distance of 1600 furlongs – (about 322 kilometres). Indicating the size of the massacre that will eventuate when Jesus takes control of this world.

At this time the inhabitants of heaven and earthly resurrected people begin to worship God in their thankfulness that God has finally taken the battle to Satan and has decisively dealt with him. God The Father has given Satan a free hand to operate as He sees fit to achieve his goal of bringing the inhabitants of this earth to subjugation to him. We must realise that God, up until this time has only dealt with him in a defensive manner. God has provided sanctuary for those who seek a living relationship with Him and the armour we need to protect ourselves from Satan.

This protection provided is a means of defence only God has ***never*** intended for us to take the fight to Satan. In the description of the armour there is no protection for our back. We have to face our enemy.

> Eph 6:10-17
>
> ***10 Finally, my brethren, be strong in the Lord, and in the power of his might.***
>
> ***11 Put on the whole armour of God, that ye may be able to stand against the wiles of the devil.***
>
> ***12 For we wrestle not against flesh and blood, but against principalities, against powers, against the***

rulers of the darkness of this world, against spiritual wickedness in high places.

13 Wherefore take unto you the whole armour of God, that ye may be able to withstand in the evil day, and having done all, to stand.

14 Stand therefore, having your loins girt about with truth, and having on the breastplate of righteousness;

15 And your feet shod with the preparation of the gospel of peace;

16 Above all, taking the shield of faith, wherewith ye shall be able to quench all the fiery darts of the wicked.

17 And take the helmet of salvation, and the sword of the Spirit, which is the word of God: KJV

Once Satan has been dealt with, the matter is settled and Christ with those that have chosen, during their lives here on earth, to have a relationship with him, will then rule the earth for 1000 thousand years. God allows the people of this earth to experience life of peace for 1000 years under Christ and then he frees Satan once more, if nothing more than to prove Satan's wickedness once and for all. When he is released (after the thousand years) he once again rounds up the people to do battle with Christ, indicating that there is nothing that will slow him down in his evil endeavours to achieve total domination through violence. For he obviously, still, believes that he will achieve his goals through violent means. So God blots out the physical realm and creates a new spiritual place (New Heaven and New Earth) where he joins us for eternity.

<u>Summation</u>

It should now be clear that the physical realm was only created that the evilness of Satan should be revealed, and we are players in this conflict, by being related to Adam. However! It is by our choice that we decide whether we continue on Satan's or God's side. God has made a way for us to get back to Him through the blood of His Son, shed on Calvary. All we have to do is reach out to Him and accept it.

<u>All done</u>

Once the outcome of determining Satan's guilt has been achieved there is no further need for the physical realm.

Gods Wonderful Love Manifest Again

We are again faced with the immense love of God that once He has achieved His goal He does not abandon us as a useless piece of residue from the battle with no further value; **no** He sets up a new Kingdom with us and comes and lives with us – not the other way around.

Rev 21:1-3

21 And I saw a new heaven and a new earth: for the first heaven and the first earth were passed away; and there was no more sea.

2 And I John saw the holy city, new Jerusalem, coming down from God out of heaven, prepared as a bride adorned for her husband.

3 And I heard a great voice out of heaven saying, Behold, the tabernacle of God is with men, and he will dwell with them, and they shall be his people, and God himself shall be with them, and be their God. KJV

This should be the hope and vision of all Christians as they go about to do the will of Christ and that the work done should be in the spirit where the salvation through Jesus Christ be taught reaching all people, so that none should perish. For when we consider the transient nature of everything around us, there cannot be any other real purpose in life

Amen.

About The Author

Edwin C. Talbot is South African-born and a dedicated Christian. He moved to Australia and worked in the Lift industry. Every day he sought the Lord's Face and His will for his life. During his Christian walk he asked God three questions, and this book is the answer to the second.

www.ingramcontent.com/pod-product-compliance
Lightning Source LLC
LaVergne TN
LVHW021738060526
838200LV00052B/3338